SWIFT REVISITED

Swift Revisited

Edited by
DENIS DONOGHUE

THE MERCIER PRESS
4 BRIDGE STREET, CORK

CONTENTS

Introduction

Every autumn, winter, and spring since September 1953, Radio Telefis Eireann has been broadcasting half-hour lectures, named in honour of Thomas Davis. Inspired by one of his famous sayings, 'Educate that you may be free,' the aim of these lectures has been to provide in popular form what is best in Irish scholarship and the sciences.

Most of the lectures have been in series; many have been single broadcasts; some have been in English, some in Irish. In the comparatively short time that has passed since they were initiated the lectures have dealt with many aspects and with many centuries of Irish social life, history, science and literature. The lecturers, distinguished for their special learning at home and abroad, have been drawn from many nations but mainly from Ireland.

The general titles of some of the series provide an idea of the variety and scope of the lectures: *The Celts; The Integrity of Yeats; The Irish at War; The Yeats We Knew; Leaders and Workers; Early Irish Poetry* and *The Years of the Great Test.*

The talks included here were delivered in 1967.

The Life of Jonathan Swift

by ROGER MCHUGH

Jonathan Swift was born in Dublin on November 30, 1667. He was (or, some think, was alleged to be) the posthumous child of Jonathan Swift, a minor law official of the King's Inns, Dublin. There are some unusual things about his childhood; when he was a baby of a year old, he was brought to England, while his mother remained in Ireland; and when, a year or two later, he was brought back to Ireland, his mother departed to England. Again, although his parents were poor, young Jonathan was sent to Kilkenny Grammar school and then to Trinity College. One of his uncles paid for this education, the best obtainable in Ireland; yet Jonathan later said of him, 'He gave me the education of a dog.' Such riddles have helped to add to the enigmas of Swift which are part of the fascination of his character.

He was at Trinity College, Dublin, from 1682 to 1686. Trinity, of course, was then the only Irish University, exclusively Protestant and mainly concerned with the training of clergymen; its students numbered only a few hundred, its system was strictly classical, Latin was the medium of instruction. The Provost was Narcissus Marsh, well-remembered in Dublin as the founder of Marsh's Library. Swift did not like him, and indeed in writing about him showed something of that pointed irony for which he is famous; the Provost, he wrote, 'has the reputation of the most profound and universal learning; this is the general opinion, neither can it be easily disproved. An old rusty iron chest in a banker's shop, strongly locked and wonderfully heavy, is full of gold; this is the general opinion, neither can it be disproved, provided the key be lost...'

Clearly this teen-ager already possessed a formidable wit and style. He seems to have cultivated both by reading much history and poetry, for it is to these interests that he himself attributed his neglect of formal study. He obtained his B.A. degree only by a special concession and a later Provost acidly remarked that Swift was 'remarkable for nothing else but making a good fire.' At any rate, he graduated in 1685, when he was eighteen – as he had entered Trinity when he was only fourteen, this is not so surprising – and he stayed on for a year, intending to take his Master's degree. At this point the Civil War in England seemed likely to spread to Ireland and Swift left for England.

In 1689 he was at Moor Park in Surrey in the household of Sir William Temple, a prominent Whig statesman and a man of considerable learning. Sir William's father, Sir John Temple, had been Master of the Rolls in Ireland before Swift's birth. In the Temple household, Swift acted as secretary to Sir William and also as tutor to a little girl named Esther Johnson. This girl, who was only eight years old when Swift met her, was allegedly the daughter of one of

Temple's stewards, but there is some evidence that she was in fact Sir William's illegitimate daughter. She is best remembered by the name which Swift gave her, Stella.

During the next few years, Swift took his Master's degree at Oxford, was ordained and worked as a curate in Kilroot, Co. Antrim. From 1696/97 he was back at Moor Park, where he wrote his first books, *A Tale of a Tub* and *An Account of a Battle between the Ancient and the Modern Books*. Both raised Swift's literary reputation, although *A Tale in a Tub* was later to sink his political fortunes. The *Battle of the Books* arose out of a literary controversy which had begun in the heyday of a distant relative of Swift, John Dryden, about the respective merits of ancient and modern writers. Dryden had tried to settle it in his *Essay of Dramatic Poesy* (1668) but thirty years later it was still a live issue in cultivated English circles. Classicists like Sir William Temple felt that the new scientific trend in writing was ruining eloquence and reverence for antiquity; while scientific writers like John Locke were throwing doubts upon the value of a classical education. Swift cast the controversy into the form of a fight between the books in St. James's Library and defended with incisiveness and grace the sweetness and light of classical literature. *A Tale of a Tub* was intended to be a defence of Anglicanism and an attack on religious fanaticism; it was written in a digressive manner which enabled Swift to satirise many foolish and vicious practices. As he did not exempt certain aspects of the Establishment from his ridicule, he was regarded thereafter by many of its supporters as a dangerous man. Literary people, then as now, admired the skill with which Swift satirised fanatical clerics, venal judges and corrupt politicians, and the ironic gravity with which he supported his argument that all unusual people are mad.

Both books were published in 1704. Meanwhile Swift became chaplain to Dublin Castle and was appointed vicar of Laracor, Co. Meath. The duties of his parish were light; sometimes, it is said, his congregation consisted only of his parish clerk, Roger Cox, and Swift's sermons began, 'Dearly beloved Roger...' He also acted as a prebend of St. Patrick's Cathedral. He sometimes visited England for long periods but from 1700 to 1707 lived mainly in Ireland. During these years Esther Johnson, attended by a relative of Sir William Temple, Rebecca Dingley, came to live in Ireland. Temple had died in 1699 after entrusting her to Swift's care. She was then in her twenties, Swift some fourteen years older. The two ladies lived in lodgings in Dublin and in Laracor, sometimes moving into the rectory when Swift was away. They followed the same procedure later, when Swift was Dean of St. Patrick's.

The decade from 1707 saw the rise of Swift's political influence. Queen Anne was on the English throne. She had renounced the rights of the Crown to a share of the first year's revenue from English benefices. Swift went to London to petition her to extend this concession to the Protestant Church of Ireland. This involved a certain amount of lobbying among the politicians. A Whig government was in power but Anne had begun to mistrust it. Swift, through Temple, had been connected with the Whigs but was now inclining towards the Tory party, which was traditionally supported by the country squires and parsons, partly because they feared the influence of the big landowners and of the new commercial interests who backed the Whigs. Swift's literary reputation now grew through his friendship with Addison and Steele; both of these, like all prominent writers of the time, had political connections and it was not long before the prominent Tory politicians were enlisting Swift's aid in the service of the party. He was put in charge of the Tory paper, *The Examiner,* and set about discrediting the Whig party by a series of articles and pamphlets. Some of these were pointed attacks upon prominent Whig party-leaders: thus he wrote of the Earl of Wharton: 'He has three predominant passions, which you will seldom observe in the same man, as arising from different dispositions of mind and naturally thwarting each other: these are love of power, love of money, and love of pleasure: They ride him sometimes by turns and sometimes all together.' Others were attacks upon Whig tactics and jobbery. But the most effective of his writings were aimed at the Whigs' favoured military leader, Sir Winston Churchill's ancestor, the Duke of Marlborough, whose costly military victories on the continent against the French, Swift demonstrated, were really enriching Marlborough himself and were playing into the hands of England's ally and traditional trade rival, Holland.

These writings appeared at a time when there was widespread uneasiness in England at the expensiveness of the war against France and at the domination of government by the Marlborough faction. The Tories used them to bring down the Whig government in 1711 and Swift's friends and associates were in power; he was now a man of great influence, the intimate not only of the great men of the literary set – Pope, Addison, Steele, Gay and the rest – but of the leading statesmen. Naturally this country parson, intelligent, able, of strong character and dominating personality, who had passed from the periphery of power to its centre, had high expectations; a bishopric seemed not unlikely. Yet he was obviously too intelligent to trust any political party completely: 'They call me nothing but Jonathan', he wrote after dining with the new Ministers, 'and I said, I believe they would leave me Jonathan, as they found me, and that I never knew a Ministry do anything for those whom they make companions of their pleasures; and I believe you will find it so; but I care not.'

He wrote these words in his *Journal to Stella.* They were, in a way, prophetic; the memory of *A Tale of a Tub* and the pressure of Swift's enemies blocked the bishopric. But there was a substantial consolation prize, the Deanship of St. Patrick's Cathedral in Dublin. It came in 1713, and just in time. The death of Queen Anne in 1714 meant the end of Tory power. The Whigs were instrumental in bringing in the German dynasty of the Hanoverians, and since George I knew no English, the Whigs controlled him: so the usual process of penalizing displaced political opponents followed; the knives were sharpened, the 'malicious toads', as Swift called the Whigs, were in full croak, and Swift was suddenly cut off from political power in England. He may not really have cared about the bishopric, but he certainly cared about this. He left England, regarded himself as going into exile and, fifteen years later, wrote to his friend Bolingbroke that it seemed he would die in Ireland 'in a rage, like a poisoned rat in a hole'.

Suppose Swift had died in 1713, the year of his installation as Dean of St. Patrick's, when he was forty-six. He would still have made a considerable impact upon men's minds and memories, both as a personality and because of his writings, including the *Journal to Stella,* a unique record of his affection for Esther Johnson and of his worth as a friend, as well as a fascinating chronicle of what went on behind the scenes of contemporary politics. It does not solve the mystery of his relationship with Stella and with the other Esther, Esther van Homrigh, the Vanessa of Swift's enigmatic poem *Cadenus and Vanessa*, which he wrote about that time. We still do not know for certain whether he married Stella or not, whether he was consanguineous with her through the Temples or not, or why he broke Vanessa's heart. In politics he would have been remembered in 1713 as the writer who had overturned a government. But he would not have been ranked among the world's greatest satirists nor would he have acquired a specially Irish connotation.

The truth is that it is to those last thirty years Swift's most enduring work belongs, both in literature and in politics, and it might never have been accomplished if he had not been forced into what he regarded as exile. For, being cut off from influence at the centre of power, as many great men from Milton to Pandit Nehru discovered, at least gives a man time to write; so *Gulliver's Travels* had time to mature. Also when a man is familiar with what goes on at the centre of power, it enables him to discern the kind of political writing which can exert most influence on the periphery of power; that is, if he cares to become involved.

At first Swift did not want to become involved. He concentrated upon being an efficient Dean of St. Patrick's and on preaching to his parishioners what he called 'plain, honest stuff'. I do not think that the parochial aspect of Swift has received until recently quite the attention it deserves; for almost fifty years he was a practising Protestant clergyman and I have no doubt that the fierce indignation which lacerated his heart had something to do with every sincere clergyman's continual struggle to remedy or to counter the effects of vice and folly. But the ironical thing is, that it was his concentration upon his parishioners' needs which brought Swift into the political arena again. For many of his parishioners were the Dublin weavers of the Coombe, descendants of Huguenots who had fled from religious persecution in France. These were very directly affected by something going on at the centre of British power; the operation of a mercantilist policy which, in simple terms, meant that the colonies of England, whether Irish or American, were expected to serve the interests of English manufacturers, traders and merchants and to subordinate their own. The operation of this policy caused a ban on the export of Irish woollens to England or abroad. Hence the weavers were badly hit. This led to Swift's pamphlet *A Proposal for the Universal Use of Irish Manufacture in Clothes and Furniture of Houses etc., Utterly Rejecting and Renouncing Everything Wearable that comes from England.* Here was a double-edged weapon of self-sufficiency and boycott which was to be used with effect by later generations of Irishmen. In 1720, when it was published anonymously, Waters the printer was prosecuted, but the Dublin jury refused to convict him; clearly, six years after Swift had quitted the English political scene, he was beginning to affect political thinking in Ireland.

This pamphlet was the first of many political writings by Swift which were directed against British policy in Ireland. The *Drapier's Letters* are famous not only for their style but for their effects; the immediate effect of defeating a gross political job and the psychological effect of promoting a temporary unity between the Anglo-Irish colonists and the Irish people. The hostile Primate Boulter wrote: 'I find that the people of every religion, country and party are alike set against Wood's halfpence and that their agreement in this city (of Dublin) has had a most unhappy influence in bringing on intimacies between Papists and Jacobites and the Whigs, who before had no correspondence with them.' Later Irish political thinkers were to invoke the name of Swift when developing the theme of national unity.

Of course Swift could not have foreseen this, nor would he necessarily have liked it. He regarded the Catholic majority as harmless, 'by the wisdom of our laws', as he put it, 'and their own want of power'. He regarded the Irish Presbyterians as a menace; since they had some land and influence, he thought that they could 'divide the Protestants by their cunning'. So he saw no injustice in those sectarian laws which blocked the advancement of both. But his insistence on the right of Ireland to be ruled justly, under the British Crown, by the Lords and Commons of *Ireland* undoubtedly helped to found the idea of Protestant colonial independence upon which Grattan built his claim for Irish legislative independence in the 1780s. When Swift wrote that 'in reason all government without the consent of the governed is the very definition of slavery', he had the Protestant colonists of Ireland in mind; but all great aphorisms have wings and this one was to fly from Ireland to America, from America to France and from France back to Ireland, where Wolfe Tone and the United Irishmen harnessed its strength to the democratic and separatist idea. So Swift, champion of the Dublin weavers, eventually was woven himself into the tapestry of the Irish national tradition. 'The woven figure cannot undo its thread'.

We can observe the same process occurring in those writings of Swift which bear more closely upon the

Irish social set-up of his time, such as his Dublin sermons and tracts. At first his view of the misery of the Irish poor is that it is due firstly to their own shiftlessness, superstition and vice, secondly to the rapacity and neglect of heartless landlords. Gradually his emphasis shifts from the first to the second cause. His most famous writing against the landlords was *A Modest Proposal for preventing the children of poor people from being a burthen to their parents or country, and for making them beneficial to the public.* It is a wonderful example of ironical shock-therapy. All cottagers, labourers and most farmers in Ireland, Swift argued, are beggars, and their children, who inevitably will grow up to be beggars too, will become a domestic and a public burden; keep a small proportion of them alive, for breeding purposes; kill off the rest when they are one year old, and eat them. This shocking proposal is made with an air of bland benevolence and of public concern; plump children make excellent food, which will increase the custom of taverns and of butchers; the project will be an excellent inducement to matrimony and will lower the illegitimate birth-rate; the poor people of Ireland at long last will own something of value; and the gentry of Ireland will be properly fed, especially the landlords, 'who, as they have already devoured most of the parents', wrote Swift, 'seem to have the best title to the children.' So from an ambush of benevolence, he springs upon the real object of attack, the landlords.

The very force of this attack, its scathing and destructive power, perhaps blinds us to the constructive thought which underlies it; for in its concluding passages Swift suggests positive remedies: 'I desire the reader will observe that I calculate my remedy for this one individual Kingdom of Ireland, and for no other that ever was, is, or, I think, ever can be upon earth. Therefore let no man talk to me of other expedients: of taxing our absentees at five shillings a pound: of using neither clothes nor household furniture, except what is of our own growth and manufacture... of quitting our animosities and factions... of teaching landlords to have at least one degree of mercy towards their tenants...' In short, he is really harping on the theme of his earlier Irish pamphlets, self-sufficiency, unity and justice. These positive ideas were repeatedly propounded in his sermons, in his *Short View of the State of Ireland* and in other Irish writings. They had little effect on Whig policy in Swift's time but lived on to influence Henry Grattan, Wolfe Tone, Thomas Davis, John Mitchel, Michael Davitt and others who shaped the later currents of Irish social thinking. Grattan and Davis invoked him as a patriot; his pamphleteering style helped to barb the pens of Tone, of Mitchel and, I suspect, of James Fintan Lalor; Davitt saw in him the initiator of the moral force movement in Ireland which set the headline for the boycotts of the Land War. He was even claimed, in our own time, to have been the first Sinn Feiner.

The figure in the tapestry changes in different lights: but it did so in Swift's time. His Irish context is different from his English context. In England he had been the great party-champion, in Ireland he became a popular champion; the Dean, a man who was guarded by Dublin workmen and who was not betrayed when a large sum was offered for the discovery of the Drapier; whose birthday was celebrated in the cities and who was regarded with particular affection in Dublin; for he helped the poor tradesmen with interest-free loans, persuaded Esther Johnson to endow one Dublin hospital and left his own money to found another for the mentally afflicted. Thus in Dublin at any rate one cannot but be conscious of the philanthropic aspect of Swift's character.

Many commentators on Swift have stressed his misanthropy. Certainly he hated the vice and folly of mankind *en masse*, anticipating Ezra Pound's reflection:

> When I consider the curious habits of dogs
> I conclude that man is the superior animal.
> When I consider the curious habits of man
> I confess, my friend, I am puzzled.

Swift did not overestimate the power of human reason, as many men of the Age of Reason did. He regarded man, as he said, as

> 'A mingled mass of good and bad;
> The best and worst that may be had'

And he lashed vice and folly unmercifully with his ironic scorn. *Gulliver's Travels* lifted his name into a universal context, that of great satire. Children still read certain parts of it in the nursery as a wonder-tale, and children are the best judges of wonder-tales, while intelligent people find that its satire applies with deadly accuracy to this atomic and space-haunted world, so it has the kind of double permanence achieved by very few literary works. Behind it, as behind the *Modest Proposal*, is that positive sense of human values which all great satirists possess and which is the fountain-head of their indignation and of their laughter. Perhaps because Swift's epitaph speaks of fierce indignation and a lacerated heart, we remember the indignation and forget the laughter. But the laughter of the comic spirit is a great solvent of rage; it provides, not an escape-hatch into complacency, but a permanent view from the moon. It is a liberating force.

And the epitaph speaks also of liberty, as if it were the chief thing for which Swift wished to be remembered: 'abi viator et imitare si poteris strenuum pro virili libertatis vindicatorem'. 'Go traveller and imitate if you can a strenuous defender of manly liberty.' Perhaps the liberty of laughter is implied as well as political liberty. It is true that when he wrote that epitaph he seemed to have little to laugh about. Both Stella and Vanessa were dead: Swift had outlived most of his literary friends; the state of Ireland seemed to him to be absolutely desperate and, as he wrote to Bolingbroke in a bad mood, he was pining away there. Yet when he was sixty-four, he could jest at death itself in his *Verses on the Death of Dr. Swift*. In these, as in many of his poems and letters, there is a spirit of characteristic ironic gaiety:

> He gave the little wealth he had
> To build a House for Fools and Mad;
> And show'd by one satiric touch,
> No Nation wanted it so much:
> That Kingdom he hath left his Debtor,
> I wish it soon may have a Better.

Six years later, in 1745, he died. Now he rests in St. Patrick's Cathedral, near the tomb of Stella and near the famous epitaph, which Yeats was to put into English verse, and from which he borrowed, I am sure, a phrase for his own; 'Horseman, pass by.' In both there is the sense of public address from the tomb and of the transience of life. Both are essentially dramatic.

And of course the fact that Yeats echoes Swift indicates the dramatic impact which Swift has had upon writers. Yeats's tower was haunted by Swift; in his middle years he saw him as a symbol of integrity, of certain intellectual and moral values of the Irish Protestant mind; he was interested in his enigmatic character and actions. Was he mad or inspired, 'beating at his breast in sybilline frenzy'? What was the real nature of his relationship with the two women, Stella and Vanessa, who in turn followed him to Ireland? Yeats tried to solve the riddle in his play, *The Words upon the Window-pane*, one of many plays about Swift. In Joyce's *Finnegans Wake* there are many allusions to him; here too he appears as the enigmatic lover, and also as the writer who dons various disguises; and this is particularly appropriate, for there is, I think, a direct line from Swift's more digressive writings through Sterne to Joyce himself, Jim the Penman, the Dublin word-weaver who wove Swift into his tipsy tapestry of sound.

Here I can but mention the enigmas which have added so much to the fascination of Swift's character, for my task is introductory and biographical. I cannot echo the words of Eliot's Fourth Tempter in *Murder in the Cathedral* and proclaim

> ...'that there was no mystery
> About this man who played a certain part in history.'

Mystery is part of Swift's attraction. And it seems to me that something of the mystery of his character is revealed by his own Beckett-like statement: 'Life is not a farce, it is a ridiculous tragedy, which is the worst kind of composition.'

Gulliver's Travels

by MATTHEW HODGART

'An immense genius; an awful downfall and ruin. So great a man he seems to me, that thinking of him is like thinking of an empire falling.' That is Thackeray's famous description of Swift; and although it may be an exaggerated account of Swift's fall – he never fell lower than to the Deanship of St. Patrick's – it does convey a sense of his greatness, his tragic frustrations and of the essentially political nature of his work. It has been usual to discuss Swift's masterpiece *Gulliver's Travels* in terms of his neurotic personality, his misanthropy, his religious and ethical views, but these seem to be less important than his politics. Swift was after all a very active and dedicated politician for many years of his long life. At first a Whig, with strong connexions with the great Whig lords, he went over to the Tories in 1710, and became the intimate friend and helper of the ministers Harley and Bolingbroke. He was a most successful propagandist, defending the government in his periodical the *Examiner*; and by his pamphlet The *Conduct of the Allies* he helped to win over the House of Commons and the public to accepting the Peace of Utrecht. With the fall of the Tories in 1714 he retreated into silence and exile for several years, but his political hand did not lose its cunning. In the 1720's he returned to the battle and in the *Drapier's Letters* took up a specifically Irish cause. Single-handed he defeated the English government over a matter of currency reform, and became a hero of the disaffected Dubliners. This work was a reversion to the cruder methods and forms of Restoration satire, including the satirical ballad, and worked very effectively in a revolutionary situation. But paradoxically his greatest creation, *Gulliver's Travels*, had no perceptible influence on the political scene of 1726. Prime Minister Walpole was not in the slightest degree shaken, although readers ever since have been shaken, as well as delighted and baffled, by this explosion of wit and misanthropy. *Gulliver* is the most striking example of a work of close and detailed political reference failing to succeed as a tract for the times. This was probably because Swift held an almost impossible political position: he belonged to the Anglo-Irish ascendancy, and as a dignitary of the established Church was a committed anti-Catholic and anti-Jacobite. Yet at the same time he was a Tory, and hated the Revolution settlement, the Williamite and Hanoverian succession, and the Whig masters of England. This was a razor-edge position, just possible to maintain during the last years of Queen Anne, but out of the question during the 1720s. Consequently Swift could only fall back into baffled rage and despair.

'I have finished my Travels,' he wrote to Charles Ford on 14th August 1725, 'and I am now transcribing them; they are admirable things, and will wonderfully mend the world.' These words, like almost everything Swift wrote, are ironical; he knew only too well that a world like this could not be mended by a book. But Swift makes it clear that he had a serious moral and political purpose behind his extravaganza, which is the expression of his mature views on life. The vehicle he chose for his purpose was not a new one: the imaginary and fantastic voyage, used for satirising institutions and attacking popular prejudices, goes back to Lucian, and is found in More's *Utopia*, Rabelais' *Gargantua*, and in the *Voyage dans la lune* (1657) by Cyrano de Bergerac. From the last two Swift probably took the notion of relative sizes, which he uses so brilliantly. Swift improves on those earlier satires by writing a close pastiche of the travel-books of his period: he catches to perfection the grave, matter-of-fact style in which William Dampier, claimed as cousin by Lemuel Gulliver, describes the marvels of the South Seas. Books like Dampier's *Voyage round the World* (1697) and Woodes Rogers' *A Cruising Voyage round the World* (1712) were widely read, and were deliberately imitated by Defoe in his *Robinson Crusoe* (1719) in the hope of producing a non-fiction best-seller. Swift, probably taking a hint or two from Defoe, goes through the same delightful pretence of telling a true story. He was not such a very stupid Irish bishop who gave the matter careful deliberation before concluding that *Gulliver's Travels* contained a pack of lies.

The book is not, however, a novel, but a political and ethical tract, which starts with a satire on English politics and concludes with a general indictment of human nature. When the French translator apologised for omitting several passages not suitable for France, Swift replied: 'If the volumes of Gulliver were designed only for the British Isles, that traveller ought to pass for a very contemptible writer. The same vices and the same follies reign everywhere; at least in the civilized countries of Europe: and the author who writes only for one city, one province, one kingdom or even one age, does not deserve to be read, let alone translated.' The phrase about vices and follies gives us a key to the structure. Book I (Lilliput) is about folly, shown in bad government: the Lilliputians have a few virtues, and are even Utopian at one point. Book II (Brobdingnag) is an exposition of good government: in contrast to the amiable and sensible giants, mankind is seen as petty and vicious. Book III returns to folly: the Laputans have almost entirely lost their wits in the pursuit of scientific speculation. The climax is reached in Book IV: the Houyhnhnms represent virtue, the Yahoos total depravity. They are the poles of behaviour that the human race is capable of attaining.

Into this framework Swift inserted many detailed references to the England of his day, which he asks us to take seriously:

> Though the present age may understand well enough the little hints we give, the parallels we draw and the characters we describe, yet this will all be lost to the next. However if these papers... should happen to live till our grandchildren are men, I hope they may have curiosity enough to

consult annals and compare dates, in order to find out.

Book I is a close allegory of the political events of the last years of Queen Anne's reign and the first years of George I's. This allegory is carefully disguised and with good reason. In the 1720's it was dangerous to attack prominent men and especially Royalty in too open a manner; with the publication of the *Drapier's Letters* Swift had already risked losing his liberty. Swift sailed as close to the wind as he dared in depicting home politics as a struggle between High Heels and Low Heels, religious controversy as a dispute about the right end to break an egg. Blefuscu or France supports the Bigendian or Roman Catholic exiles; the heir to the throne has a tendency to High Heels, just as the Prince of Wales favoured the Opposition; Flimnap-Walpole capers along the tightrope of political jobbery. These identifications are obvious, but in the figure of Gulliver there is a deeper allegory. Except for the moment when he puts out the fire, Gulliver is not Swift but Swift's friend Bolingbroke, and sometimes an amalgam of Bolingbroke and Harley. The story is taken to 1714, when Bolingbroke was threatened with impeachment for treasonable correspondence with the Pretender and fled to France. The point of this interpretation is that Swift was not the complete egoist that some critics have seen in him: rather than expressing his many personal disappointments in a mood of self-pity, he is sending a message of loyalty to his friends in trouble. Brobdingnag is largely a political Utopia – England as it might have been if the Tories had remained in power. Swift is being realistic here, implying that if Englishmen could not become Houyhnhnms they could at least be like the Brobdingnagians, who though rather repulsive when you look at them too closely are basically sound in their politics. Swift took politics to be an essential part of the good life, and venerated the memory of his patron Sir William Temple, who may be represented in the King of Brobdingnag. The King is also a Tory mouthpiece: some of the things he denounces, a 'mercenary standing army in the midst of peace, and among a free people,' and the National Debt were common objects of Tory attack. But it goes beyond party ideas: the basis of the Brobdingnagian state is the humanist principle 'that whoever could make two Ears of Corn, or two Blades of Grass grow upon a Spot of Ground where only one grew before, would deserve better of mankind and do more essential Service to his Country, than the whole Race of Politicians put together.' Finally, the Brobdingnagians possess the gift that Swift valued most, the perfect prose style, 'clear, masculine, and smooth', a style which is seen to perfection in the Book itself.

The third voyage was written last of the four, and is the least effective as satire or imaginative creation. Laputa, the Flying Island, is the Court and Government of George I, which keeps England and Ireland in subjection. The revolt of Lindalino (Dublin) was an incident so dangerously topical that it was suppressed in the early editions. The Laputans fail to crush this revolt because they are afraid of the combustible fuel directed at the island's adamantine bottom: a direct allegory of Swift's *Drapier's Letters*, by which he had just won a signal victory over the English Government. The Laputans are typically English in their love of political intrigue (as Swift wrote to Stella from London, 'the rabble here are much more inquisitive in politics than they are in Ireland') and in their love of music, a reference to the keen dispute between the supporters of Italian Opera and of Handel in the 1720's. The centre-piece of the satire is the Academy of Projectors, which is partly directed at the scientists of the Royal Society and the Dublin Philosophical Society. It must not be assumed that Swift was completely philistine about science: as we have seen, he admired the practical inventor who could grow two ears of corn where one grew before, which is in accordance with the Baconian aims of the Royal Society. He certainly knew more about science than most literary men have done. This is shown by his close parody of scientific papers, based on careful reading of the *Transactions* of the Royal Society. But he considered scientific speculation as secondary to the main business of man upon earth, which is right conduct. There were less worthy reasons for his attitude: he saw the great Newton mainly as a Whig politician who had been called in by the Government for support over 'Wood's Halfpence', and he resented the lack of patronage now given to men of letters, as compared with the great days of Queen Anne. Finally the word 'projector' meant not so much a scientist, for which the usual eighteenth-century word was 'virtuoso' as a promoter of get-rich-quick schemes. Swift is also satirizing the speculative financial projects which were floated in large numbers in the six years before 1720, when the greatest of them, the South Sea Bubble, burst.

The Strudbrugs, the immortals who live on in senility, are a magnificent invention in Swift's most macabre vein; but as a whole the satire in Book III is too diffuse, and the resentment is more like irritation than *saeva indignatio*.

The Fourth Book, in which Gulliver encounters the rational horses and the appallingly irrational Yahoos, presents much more serious difficulties. It is one of the few outstanding works of the imagination over which the most intelligent readers seem to be in hopeless disagreement. This is the case also with *Hamlet* and *Waiting for Godot*, both of which Book IV incidentally resembles in its total pessimism and black wit. The effect is so complex that we must conclude that Swift was saying more than he intended; but his intentions are far from clear. Is he writing from an orthodox Christian standpoint, and offering the Yahoos as examples of Original Sin? Are the horses really meant to embody Swift's ideals, or do they stand for ethical attitudes that he means to satirize? At the end of the story, has Gulliver gone mad, or is he the only sane man in a mad world? Is Swift himself a half-crazy misanthrope, or is he simply telling the truth about the human condition? These are only some of the questions that have been raised by the critics, and in my opinion no simple answer can be given to any of them.

Now, Book IV is still concerned with politics, although the argument has moved from the particular to the general. Whereas Book II contains a stock Tory attack on standing armies, Swift now offers a general indictment of war in absolute terms. Against the complacent ideas about colonisation widely held in his time, Swift opposes his perception of the naked truth, in his most startling reductive language:

> For instance, a Crew of Pirates are driven by a Storm they know not whither; at length a Boy discovers Land from the Top-mast; they go on Shore to rob and plunder; they see an harmless People, are entertained with Kindness, they give the country a new Name, they take formal possession of it for the King, they set up a rotten plank or a Stone for a Memorial, they murder two or three Dozen of the Natives, bring away a Couple more by Force for a Sample, return home, and get their Pardon. Here commences a new Dominion acquired with a Title by *Divine Right*. Ships are sent out with the first Opportunity; the Natives driven out or destroyed, the Princes tortured to discover their Gold; a free Licence given to all Acts of Inhumanity and Lust; the Earth reeking with the Blood of its inhabitants; and this execrable Crew of Butchers employed in so pious an Expedition, is a modern Colony sent to convert and civilize idolatrous and barbarous People.

In this marvellous tirade Swift seems to have forgotten – or has he? – that such things had happened in Ireland during the centuries before him, and that Ireland was still in a sense an English colony. In these and other parts of the book, as where he indicts all lawyers and Law root and branch, Swift has shifted from attacks on particular English governments and policies to the total rejection of all government – the horses do very well without any – and that comes close to the doctrine of anarchism. It is striking that the philosophical anarchist William Godwin quotes Book IV of *Gulliver's Travels* with approval, in support of his argument that all political institutions are totally corrupt; and it is paradoxical that the great Tory High-churchman should have reached so subversive a position.

The main field of Book IV is, however, ethics rather than politics; and it is certain that the horses were intended to embody Swift's ethical ideals. They represent the kind of stoicism that Swift advocates elsewhere, a philosophy shared by many eighteenth-century writers. Stoicism means the pursuit of human happiness by living according to Nature, by following the light of reason and by unremitting industry; above all, it means control of the passions, and especially of the most degrading passion, the fear of death. The Houyhnhnms are naturally good, but, guided by nature and reason, they work hard to achieve their happiness. They 'train up their Youth to Strength, Speed and Hardiness' by exercise and cold baths – the education of the foals is a strange prophecy of the English Public

School system. The horses seek no reward in heaven, and their final reward on earth is freedom from Struldbrugian fears. 'If they can avoid casualties, they die only of old Age, and are buried in the obscurest Places that can be found, their Friends and Relations expressing neither Joy nor Grief at their Departure; nor does the dying Person discover the least Regret that he is leaving the World, any more than if he were returning home from a Visit to one of his Neighbours. About ten Days before their Death, which they seldom fail in computing, they return the Visits that have been made by those who are nearest in the Neighbourhood... they take a solemn Leave of their Friends, as if they were going to some remote part of the Country, where they designed to pass the rest of their lives.' I find no hint of irony at the horses' expense in that moving passage, and no trace of Christian doctrine. The Houyhnhnms are what men could be if they lived reasonably, the Yahoos what men will become if they are not controlled by a strict but human morality.

But if that was Swift's design, as I believe it to have been, it has become obscured by several contradictory shades of meaning, which can be traced to Swift's experience and deepest feelings. In the first place, the Yahoos physically resemble the Irish peasantry, among whom Swift travelled just before writing this book. He writes in a letter: 'the poorer sort of our natives... live in the utmost ignorance, barbarity and poverty, giving themselves wholly up to idleness, nastiness and thievery.' Can nothing be done, he asks, 'to reduce this uncultivated people from that idle, savage, beastly, thievish manner of life?' Thus he describes Ireland; 'the whole kingdom a bare face of nature, without horses or plantations; filthy cabins, miserable half-starved creatures, *scarce in human shape*.' Now it is striking that Swift does not blame the Irish peasants for being Yahoos, but traces the cause to 'the poverty and slavery they suffer from, their inhuman neighbours and the base corrupt spirits of too many of the chief gentry etc.' That is a correct diagnosis of the miseries of Ireland, where the English and Anglo-Irish landlords, often absentees, were the villains. Now, if the Yahoos physically correspond to the peasantry, the master Houyhnhnms must correspond in some way with the upper classes, and this is indeed the case. They are aristocratic in their cold good manners and haughty disdainfulness, as when Gulliver

> took a second Leave of my Master: But as I was going to prostrate myself to kiss his Hoof, he did me the Honour to raise it gently to my Mouth. I am not ignorant how much I have been censured for mentioning this last Particular. Detractors are pleased to think it improbable, that so illustrious a Person should descend to give so great a Mark of Distinction to a Creature so inferior as I.

The horse is the perfect symbol of upper-class culture. Your knight is a horseman, chevalier, caballero; Caligula made his horse a consul, and why not, since racing is the sport of kings? England is again ruled by a horse-loving Queen, with her Houyhnhnms courtiers, its Society held together by a network of Hunts and Pony Clubs. When the Duke of Wellington was asked if he was an Irishman, he replied, 'if I were born in a stable, would that make me a horse?' Of course it would, and a good Irishman too; for in Ireland the gentry's cult of horseflesh is at its most intense, and there, Swift assures us in *A Modest Proposal*, men are by no means 'as fond of their *Wives*, during the Time of their Pregnancy, as they are now of their *Mares* in Foal.' It would seem, therefore, that Swift's attitude to the Yahoos and to the Houyhnhnms is complicated by his mixed feelings – of love and hate – about the political and social structure of eighteenth-century Ireland.

Swift was always uncertain about his social standing, and I think that some unconscious class-feeling colours the details of Book Four. He had identified himself with an aristocratic position in politics; he venerated his patron Sir William Temple and later the Tory ministers; yet his relations with great men were often marked, as Dr Johnson shrewdly observed, by 'petulance and obtrusion', which 'are rarely produced by magnanimity'. On one occasion Swift wrote to Stella that he had warned Bolingbroke 'never to appear cold to me, for I would not be treated like a schoolboy: that I had felt too much of that in my life already' (meaning from Sir William Temple), and in an even more revealing passage, 'Don't you remember how I used to be in pain when *Sir William Temple* would look cold and out of humour for 3 or 4 days, and I used to suspect a hundred reasons. I have pluckt up my spirit since then, faith; but he spoiled a fine gentleman.' So strongly did Swift feel about the snubs he had endured, that despite his intentions he produced in the Houyhnhnms a distorted image of the great gentleman in whose company he had lived but of whose caste he could never be.

The phrase 'treated like a schoolboy' gives the key to another side of the Houyhnhnms; they are adult, all too adult. As grown-ups are supposed to be, they are rational, disciplined and clean; but they are also distant and cold. The Yahoos, on the other hand, are horribly infantile: like most children they enjoy playing with dirt and are hideously irrational in their desires. The greatest shock that Gulliver receives is when he discovers himself to be one of them, although he feels himself to be a rational creature. He is banished from the island, like a naughty child from the company of stern and uncomprehending adults. His only real friends in all his travels have been his little sixty-foot nurse Glumdaïclitch, and the sorrel nag who looks after him affectionately: their parting is the most moving passage in the book:

> My Master and his Friends continued on the Shoar, till I was almost out of Sight; and I often heard the Sorrel Nag (who always loved me) crying out, *Mhuy illa nyha maiah Yahoo*, Take Care of thyself, gentle *Yahoo*.

The Portuguese sea-captain is another kind nurse, but by this time Gulliver is as obsessively mad as Don

Quixote (on whom at this point he is modelled) and cannot reconcile himself to adult humanity. It is not without good reason that *Gulliver's Travels*, suitably expurgated, has become a children's classic. The poignant and Dickensian experiences of childhood are at the heart of the book; and indeed there is a streak of childishness in much of Swift's other work, as in the 'little language' or baby-talk that he used in writing to Stella. Because of these peculiar under-currents, emotional, social and political, Book Four is inconsistent and impossible to interpret with certainty. It speaks at times with the accents of tragedy – and having seen in mass-murders of our century what human nature is capable of, we cannot say that Swift's tragic vision of the Yahoos was wholly wrong – but it also speaks to us with infinite wit and a strange gaiety. Swift's final defence against the horrors of existence was laughter.

The Dean and the Drapier

by MARK KINKEAD-WEEKES

After the collapse of the Tories in 1714, Swift came back to Ireland, an unwilling and embittered repatriate. Ireland meant exile from all he most cared for: the society of statesmen and poets; influence at the centre of things; work that was worthy of his powers. In Dublin the new Dean was isolated, lonely, unappreciated, looking back to a past that nobody around him shared or cared about. He felt bitter that no position had been found for him in English society. He was bound to pay now for his political past; to be fair game for the taunting of triumphant Whigs both in England and Ireland. He was regarded with suspicion; his mail was interfered with; his Whig Archbishop tried to limit his Decanal powers. Vowing to have nothing to do with Irish politics, he devoted six years to a series of unpublishable defences of the Tories and their policies. He was living in the past.

But in the 1720s, the 'Condition of Ireland' question recalled the old Swift in the new role of the Irish Patriot. His motives were complex. Indeed, the advantage of his new role was that it offered him more than a chance to attack old political enemies; it enabled him also to resolve some of the tensions of his personal situation. He could get rid of hatred and frustration by trying to remedy what he hated. The degrading poverty and exploitation of Ireland flayed his sensibility; but so did the factiousness, the timidity and apathy of the Irish. It is very natural to hate what one cannot help, for being so helpless. Swift's new involvement in political action allowed him to channel these complex feelings in a positive direction. Half way through the decade, he managed for a few precious years to identify himself with Ireland. He was, and would remain, a Tory, a member of the Anglo-Irish Protestant Ascendancy. But through his masquerade as the Drapier, and especially when a price was put on his head, Swift became a popular hero whom nobody would or dared betray. The Drapier-Dean could speak on behalf of, not a class or a party, but the idea of a nation.

Both personally and politically, however, the *Drapier's Letters* record only a temporary victory in a losing war. The main result of the political triumph was to force Walpole to make sure that it could not happen again. The idea of a nation proved ephemeral as the Irish relapsed into former positions and interests, factions and apathy. Behind the mask of the Drapier Swift's face had momentarily lost its sneer; but the mask had to be laid aside, and its successors would assume more horrific expressions.

The real fascination of the *Drapier's Letters* is that we watch the creation of a dramatic *fiction*. There was acted out in historical Dublin a masquerade; at its centre a Mask which could be what Swift himself could not, and could speak for what did not yet exist, the 'whole People of Ireland'. The Masquerade offered in daily life a dramatic action in which people could express their frustrations in parts which had been written for them, and which they could play in safety. But in sober and bitter truth, the masquerade was only a wish-fulfilling parenthesis, before social, political, and economic realities took over again.

As early as 1707, in his unpublished allegory *The Story of the Injured Lady*, Swift had expressed the grievance of the Irish Establishment against English exploitation. He regarded Ireland as an independent kingdom, joined to England under one Crown, but having otherwise the right to govern its own affairs. In 1720, however, the Declaratory Act 'for the better securing the Dependency of... Ireland' brutally underlined the very different view held by the English Government.

Yet the weakness of the Irish Establishment lay in the fact that they were themselves an exploiting minority, kept in control by the power of England. Their bitterness was that their own 'kith and kin' in England would not recognise them as such, or give them the same political and economic freedom of action that English subjects of the King enjoyed; but they themselves asserted a vast gulf of division from the mass of the Catholic peasantry. The Protestant Ascendancy was itself split between the English Interest and the Irish Interest, and between the Established Church and the Dissenters. So for all the outcry, when the Declaratory Act sought to remove the last ambiguities from the Dependency of Ireland, constitutional arguments about its legality did nothing to alter the facts of the power situation.

Two months after the Declaratory Act, Swift published *A Proposal for the Universal Use of Irish Manufactures.* He must have known that there was little or no chance of an effective boycott of English goods, but he set out to whip up resentment by touching, one after another, all the Irish grievances. The miscellaneous nature of the tract shows him feeling for his audience, and feeling his own way towards an effective stance. He begins to channel his own mixed emotions: 'Whoever travels this Country, and observes the *Face* of Nature, or the *Faces*, and Habits, and Dwellings of the Natives, will hardly think himself in a Land where either *Law*, *Religion*, or *common Humanity* is expressed'. As the conventional 'face of nature' modulates so sharply into the *faces* of the rural Irish, pity is fused with anger; but both are double-edged. Resentment is aroused, but it also points to the shame of those who will not help themselves. Swift is still a long way from a voice to which the whole People of Ireland would say 'Amen', but he is moving in that direction, with a sure instinct that the economic sphere is the one in which collective resistance may prove possible. When the tract was declared 'false, scandalous and seditious' and its printer prosecuted, Swift ceased to be regarded as a suspicious alien. He became reconciled to the patriots within the Irish Establishment; and the Dublin weavers, many of whom lived within sight of St. Patrick's Cathedral, began to look to Swift as their protector. His isolation was broken; he began to sense a new power and purpose.

What he needed was the right kind of issue: sufficiently black and white, offering a chance of practical success, and threatening the direct interest of a wide enough range of Irishmen. It was just this that the affair of Wood's Halfpence provided. No issue could have been clearer. The right of the King to grant a patent for Ireland's coinage could not be legally challenged; but there had been a contemptuous refusal to consult the Irish Parliament. The amount involved was excessive and the profit margin huge. It was rightly suspected that there had been corruption in the issue of the patent, and there was every reason to expect further corruption in its execution. The economic effects were bound to be disastrous. Every Irishman would be directly threatened where it hurt, in his purse. Here at last was an issue on which the Irish could be persuaded to unite. Furthermore, if an economic boycott of the new coins could be organised, it could not be branded illegal. The King had the right to grant the patent, but the law could not bind anybody to accept the money. Most important of all, the real issue was the proof of what it meant to be a colony of an exploiting power. But for that very reason, the act of economic resistance could symbolise a wider rebellion, and it could do so with impunity.

It is here that we see the significance of Swift's masquerade. He made no move until after the Irish Parliament had shown its determination to resist the patent. His efforts would have been futile if the Irish

Privy Council and the Commissioners of Revenue had not withstood English pressure to receive Wood's coins, and to pay the Army with them, ensuring their spread throughout the country. Swift did not originate the idea of the boycott, and the *Drapier's Letters* were only the most spectacular of the factors which organised public opinion to make the boycott effective. Swift's real design lay deeper; the *Letters* developed, step by step, a strategic demonstration of how a perfectly legal economic action could generate the force of treason. They are an extraordinary example of the application of irony to mass action. The Drapier taught ordinary unsubtle people the art of ironical behaviour, how to do one thing and mean another. Furthermore his success did not depend upon the number of Irishmen who consciously understood that they were acting in this double sense. To create a situation in which anyone who boycotted *might* be expressing the spirit of Independence itself, was a political masterstroke. The precise motives that led a particular Dubliner to support the Drapier no longer mattered; he could not follow the Drapier's instructions without involving himself in implicit sedition. The reaction of intelligent men who were patriotic or self-interested enough to boycott, but who did not share Swift's political implications, provides one of the most amusing sideshows in the masquerade.

The first necessity of the struggle was, however, to persuade the middle- and working-classes that they were in real danger from Wood's halfpence, that there was a remedy, and that the remedy was perfectly safe and legal. These are the objects of the pamphlet in which the Drapier first made his appearance, the *Letter to the Shopkeepers, Tradesmen, Farmers, and Common-People of Ireland*. Swift had already discovered in his *Proposal* (to which the Drapier refers in his opening remarks) the uselessness of exhortation from above. The first reason for the choice of the Mask was a matter of acceptable tone. The Drapier was exactly in the middle of the social system, and could speak to the all-important shopkeeping class, whose solidarity was essential, as one of themselves, with their own flavour of speech, their own scale of value, their own bluff common sense. The Drapier's voice was also a way of dramatising what might otherwise have seemed remote economic arguments. The consequences of Wood's Halfpence are presented in terms that come home to the experience of ordinary people; how bad coinage entails ruin for everybody, high and low; how farmers must beg and shopkeepers break and starve, because everyone depends upon his neighbour. The illustration of what to do about it is worth the whole of the *Proposal*, because his adopted role has enabled Swift to imagine economic action in really practical terms, which carry an immediate conviction of their possibility: 'For my own part, I am already resolved what to do; I have a pretty good Shop of *Irish Stuffs* and *Silks*, and instead of taking Mr. WOOD's bad Copper, I intend to Truck with my Neighbours the *Butchers*, and *Bakers*, and *Brewers* and the rest, *Goods for Goods*, and the little *Gold* and *Silver* I have, I will keep by me like my *Heart's Blood* till better Times...' The Drapier's simplest readers might not grasp the legal evidence that it is quite safe to refuse the coin, but the account is lucid, and the air of authority is thoroughly reassuring.

At the same time, from the very beginning, the voice of the Drapier allowed Swift to write on two levels. The reference to the *Proposal* is an acknowledgement that he himself is the author, and the farcical arithmetic is a deliberately characteristic Swiftian trademark – indeed rather riskily so, for the tone in these passages carried an unmistakeable note of condescension towards his role, and the ostensible audience. The simplest shopkeepers might conceivably have been impressed by the Drapier's calculations, but literary critics have been remarkably condescending themselves, in taking that as the point. In fact, from the very beginning, Swift wanted his face to be visible behind the Mask to anybody sufficiently intelligent; for as soon as it is obvious that the Drapier *is* a mask, a level of ironic implication comes into focus. Swift is already announcing, in the references to the 'gracious' King and his 'advisers', his real target. On one level the humble Drapier stands forth as Ireland's honest champion against the obscure Ironmonger. On the deeper level, Swift is already beginning to suggest that Wood's Halfpence are only the ostensible issue, though vital in itself. Using this issue, he prepares to mount Ireland's rebellion against its dependency on a corrupt Ministry, and a corrupt Court.

The Drapier's second letter, *To Mr Harding the Printer*, takes this further. On the surface it works like the first, trying to destroy the effect of the reported evidence to the English Privy Council, which seemed to bolster the English case; and to reassure ordinary people against the disturbing rumour that the King might issue a proclamation on Wood's behalf. Furthermore, the Drapier shows how the boycott can be developed from individual and private action to public and collective action. Where the first Letter played on fear, the second begins to arouse anger, and to direct it to mass protest. But the deeper level of implication is more open now, when the Drapier ironically describes how a 'great Kingdom' has been kept 'in daily Dread of utter Destruction; not by a powerful Invader at the Head of Twenty thousand Men... not by a tyrannical Prince (for we never had one more gracious) or a corrupt Administration; but by one single, diminutive, insignificant Mechanick.' 'Good God!', the ironic voice exclaims, 'Who are this Wretch's *Advisers*? Who are his *Supporters*, *Abettors*, *Encouragers*, or *Sharers*? Mr. Wood will OBLIGE me to take Five-pence Half-penny of his Brass in every Payment. And I will shoot Mr. Wood and his Deputies through the Head, like *High-way Men*, or *House-Breakers*, if they dare to force one Farthing of their coin on me...' When he describes Wood as a 'little Arbitrary *Mock-Monarch*' who dares 'prescribe what no King of England ever attempted' and 'takes upon him the Entire Legislature, and an absolute Dominion over the Properties of the Whole Nation', and still more when he cites the analogy of Hampden's stand against Charles I; the Dean behind the

Drapier is throwing down a political defiance to the monarch behind Wood, while remaining completely out of danger because his true meaning remains ironically implicit. In response to this second Letter's carefully worded sample 'Declaration', public manifestoes began to be sent in to the Irish newspapers, notably from a group of Dublin bankers.

The English Privy Council then issued its Report in favour of Wood, and the stage was set for the implicit to become explicit. The Drapier's third Letter is addressed no longer to a popular audience, but 'To the Nobility and Gentry of the Kingdom of Ireland'. His style rises because his subject has risen. Now that the English government has taken up Wood's cause, the matter has clearly become a struggle between the two Kingdoms, and an opportunity to voice Ireland's anger at the distinction so obviously drawn by the English Government between the rights of Englishmen and those of Irishmen. The Drapier rehearses former arguments about Wood and the halfpence, but the heart of his new letter is his real subject. 'WERE not the People of *Ireland* born as *free* as those of *England*? How have they forfeited their Freedom? Is not their *Parliament* as fair a *Representative* of the *People*, as that of *England*? And hath not their Privy Council as great, or a greater share in the Administration of publick Affairs? Are they not subjects of the same King? Does not the same *Sun* shine over them? And have they not the same *God* for their Protector? Am I a *Free-man* in *England*, and do I become a *Slave* in six Hours, by crossing the Channel?...'

The theme of Irish Independence is now in the open. When the Drapier reminded his readers of his plea for public Declarations, the response was spectacular, and very many of the signatories must have been availing themselves of the ironical behaviour to which the Drapier was showing the way. The economic boycott had become a political demonstration.

Swift followed up with a fourth *Letter to the Whole People of Ireland*, and this time he deliberately crossed the line which until then had separated him from sedition. He made it impossible for the newly arrived Lord-Lieutenant, his old acquaintance Carteret, to avoid arresting the printer and offering a reward for the betrayal of the author. The irony becomes more daringly personal when the Drapier defends Walpole's integrity as 'above all temptation'; when he suggests that the 'wisest and best' monarchs use their prerogative as seldom as possible; and computes how many thousand 'operatives' might be necessary to make good Walpole's threat to force Wood's brass down Ireland's throat. But one paragraph contains an open and deliberate defiance of the English claim to legislate for a dependent Ireland, while maintaining, as Swift always did, the legality of the Hanoverian succession and Ireland's subservience to the Crown. Now the implicit *political* solidarity of the Irish was put to the test. Many felt, like Archbishop King, that Swift had gone too far, but no informer appeared. Swift reminded the Grand Jury, in his *Seasonable Advice*, that to find against the printer was to find not only for Wood, but for the wolves behind him. The first Jury refused to present, and when a second Jury was empanelled they actually pronounced their verdict not against Harding, but against 'all such persons as have attempted, or shall endeavour by fraud or otherwise to Impose the... Half-pence upon us.' They had learnt their lesson in irony, for they were implicitly finding against the English Government.

So confident was Swift now that he wrote a *Letter to the Lord Chancellor Middleton* in vindication of the fourth letter, and proposed to sign it with his own name; but on a hint from Carteret through the Archbishop, he wisely decided not to go ahead, and the Letter remained unpublished until 1735. But he produced in its place his ironic masterpiece as the Drapier, the *Letter to Molesworth.* He pretends to be weary, disillusioned, and ready to quit; but as the account he gives of his biography reminds one irresistably of Swift himself, so the double identity gives to the apparent vexation a wicked, flickering impudence. Swift has brought his past into relation with his present, delightedly parodying the personal situation from which the *Drapier's Letters* had in fact rescued him. In the act of apparently apologising for having gone too far, he keeps repeating his fault. And he delights in the political unity he has forged. In addressing the Letter to Molesworth, whose Old Whig principles were as well known as his opposition to Walpole's Irish policy; and in blaming Locke, Molyneux, and Molesworth himself for his ideas, the Drapier belabours the English Whig Ministry with what was supposed to be their own political philosophy: 'Law, and Liberty, and the Common Rights of Mankind.'

When months went by and no move came from England, Swift prepared yet another Letter: *An Humble Address to both Houses of Parliament*. But this was never published, for on August 26th 1725 the news came that Wood had surrendered his patent. 'The work is done', Swift wrote, 'and there is no more need of the Drapier'.

It was a famous victory. But though the masquerade now stood as a matter of historical record, the final ironies remained to be played out, with Swift no longer in full control of them. The political unity of the Irish lasted no longer than the immediate economic self-interest that had enabled it to be brought about. Moreover, if politics is the art of power, Walpole was a consummate politician. He had been trapped into momentary defeat, but he set to work carefully and expertly to make sure that no such resistance could crystallise again. He sent over a new Primate of All Ireland with instructions to see that all significant vacancies in church and government were filled by supporters of the English Interest. So well did Hugh Boulter succeed that the affair of Wood's Halfpence was the last serious move for 'independency' in Swift's lifetime. By an exquisite twist of the knife, Wood was not only given a pension of £24,000 by way of compensation, but the money was drawn from funds in the Irish Establishment. Walpole was an ironist too, though Swift seems to have been spared the knowledge of it. What he *did* realise was, however, quite enough. The euphoria of the Drapier's masquerade went on being re-lived by the Irish, but Swift himself steadily lapsed into the bitter pessimism from which he had momentarily emerged.

At the height of his triumph, when, as Bishop Nicholson ruefully told the Archbishop of Canterbury, the Drapier-Dean was 'the Darling of the Populace, his Image and Superscription on a great many Sign-Posts in this City and other great towns', Swift was back at work on *Gulliver's Travels*, which the Drapier's performances had interrupted. 'Interrupted' seems the right word, for the mood of his greatest work goes back behind the interlude of Wood's halfpence to connect with that of the years of exile. In the *Travels* the famous victory is already seen in perspective: merely an exceptional episode in the continuing tyranny of Laputa – an episode, moreover, which the English printer carefully cut out. When Swift returned from his last visit to England in 1727, he was received as a popular hero still, and two years later the cathedral bells were set a-ringing again, and there were 'bonfires and other illuminations' as the Dean came back from a stay in the country. But a month after the reception of 1727 the popular hero was writing: 'As to politics; in England it is hard to keep out of them, and here it is a shame to be in them, unless by way of laughter and ridicule, for both of which my taste is gone. I suppose there will be as much mischief as interest, folly, ambition and faction will bring about...' Ireland was already becoming again for him 'a land of slaves, where all are fools and all are knaves'. And in 1729, after two years of disastrous harvests, the countryside had shown him a terrible vision of the 'mischief' he had foreseen from the apathy, the folly and faction of the Irish Establishment. He took up the mask of an honest economist once more; but in a way that made a savage comment on the euphoria of its predecessor, as the homely features of the Drapier gave way to the sinister blandness of the Modest Proposer. Irony is no longer a pointer to mass action, for Swift no longer deludes himself that his countrymen can act. It has turned into a whiplash, wielded without expression by a faceless man, on slavemasters and slaves alike. It is merely the logical end of exploitation that the English should eat the Irish. But it is no less true that the 'slaves' are incapable of responding effectively to those who would help them to help themselves. So, with equally brutal logic, an Irish Establishment voice modestly proposes, not 'vain, idle, visionary thoughts' like those that had motivated the Drapier, but 'something Solid and Real, of no Expence and little Trouble, full in our Power, and whereby we can incur no Danger in *Disobliging England*', the offering up to the knife, of the children of the Irish poor.

But the 'savage indignation' speaks, as indeed Swift's tombstone does, of lacerating pain as much as anger – pain at what the facts of history had made of the dramatic fiction of the Drapier and the 'Whole People of Ireland'.

Dean of St. Patrick's: A View from the Letters

by JOHN HOLLOWAY

The sorry tale of Swift's last years is well known, and I shall not dwell on it. 'I am what I am', it is said he muttered in his dotage in 1744, a year before his death. One wonders what trace there was in his mind of St. Paul in the First Corinthians: 'I am the least of the Apostles... but by the grace of God I am what I am' – with, he meant, an assurance of immortality. Swift's widowed cousin Mrs. Martha Whiteway, on whom he came to be quite dependent just before his collapse, – has a pitiful account of the crucial illness in November 1742. 'He walked in the house ten hours a day... his meat was served up ready cut, and sometimes it would lie an hour before he would touch it, and then ate it walking... the torture he was in, is not to be described.'

But I think one must see these years in proportion. Swift was then 75, his strong body survived into helpless old age, and unless we are very foolish we know that in greater or lesser degree, such things as these are part of the common lot. Old age had been coming to him for many years: old age, and also the isolation and ageing of friends that it brings. In April 1740 he complained to his cousin of excruciating pain all night – but noted that she would put it down only to gout;

which his acquaintance John Boyle, fifth Earl of Orrery, had 'settled, confirmed', though only 35. The winter of 1739-40 had been bitterly cold in Dublin. 'Our kingdom is turned out to be Muscovy, or worse... I walk only in my bedchamber and closet, which hath also a fire'. 'Still my garden is all white', he wrote a month later. He is 72. Two years before this, he lamented that he was so much out of touch, he could no longer catch the references in Pope's latest satire. The year before again, he had several times felt near enough to death, to send his most private papers to the safe keeping of friends: 'I have not been out of doors further than my Garden, for several months'. Also in 1737: 'I find such a weekly decay, that hath made it impossible for me to ride above five or six miles at furthest'; 'I have not one rag of memory left, and my friends have all forsaken me'.

But after all, he was 70. No wonder if his friends were going. That same year, he had lamented the last days of Rebecca Dingley, erstwhile companion to his lifelong friend – or more than friend – Stella Johnson: Mrs. Dingley 'quite sunk with years and unwieldiness... I do not find her nearest relations consider her in the least'. By now she was probably 70 too. Stella herself, of course, had died long before. Age was also taking some of Swift's best correspondents. Gay died in 1732 aged 67; Arbuthnot, another of the circle in Swift's London days, and physician to the old queen, early in 1735, at 68. Young Orrery's father, one of Swift's good friends (unlike the son, if truth be told) died in 1731. In that year, Swift had become estranged from his old friend the lively, dogmatic, philandering landowner Knightley Chetwode. In 1735 died his housekeeper, the 'grave Presbyterian' Mrs. Brent, whom he called Sir Robert Walpole, in honour of his most powerful opponent, ever-present to his mind. In his later years he had dined alone with her almost every evening of the week.

That was partly because his deafness made it hard for him to go much into company. It is now familiar knowledge that for many years Swift suffered from Ménière's disease, or *labyrinthine vertigo* in the middle ear; which was at that time beyond treatment or even diagnosis by medical science. He more or less knew this himself: 'I believe my disorder is particular, and out of the Experience of our Physicians here'. That fact mingled in his mind, however, with his doubts in general about Irish doctors, and his recurrent sardonic gloom. Somewhere, he says, he has the *London Dispensary*, with remedies for deafness and giddiness; 'but my books are so confused that I can not find it, nor would value it if I did'.

This illness of Swift's one must also put into perspective: painful and humiliating, but intermittent. Even as early as 1722 he was writing to Chetwode like this:

> I have been this 5 weeks... so disordered with a noise in my ears and deafness, that I am utterly unqualified for all conversation or thinking... now the disease I fear is deeper rooted, and I never stir out.

But no less than twelve years later:

> My head is every day more or less disordered by a Giddyness. Yet I ride the Strand here constantly when fair weather invites me.

And this was the year in which the younger Lord Orrery said that the Dean 'enjoys more health and Vivacity this Winter than he has felt for some years past'; and early in 1737; 'the Dean feasted his Clergy last week with Ladies, Music, Meat and Wine... as a Musician I gain'd admittance to join Chorus with *Away with Cuzzoni, away with Faustina*'. (One wishes one knew the tune of that chorus.) John Boyle, on the other hand, is not the most reliable of witnesses about Swift. But even three years later, he and Mrs. Whiteway both described Swift as in good health and spirits, and speak favourably of his hearing, though Mrs. Whiteway added that he is 'indolent in writing'. He was still well enough, at least from time to time; though by now an old man, and far from a satisfied one.

In some ways, the eighteenth century spirit nearest to Swift was Samuel Johnson. 'A world where much is to be endured, and little is to be enjoyed', Johnson wrote in *Rasselas*. This is rather how Swift saw the 'cursed factious oppressed miserable country' he lived in after 1713. Yet at the same time he knew how to enjoy that little. He more than once told his friends that he could not settle in England again; not on any terms likely to come his way. With his indifferent health, he valued the comfort, and the circumstance, of his Deanery. In 1732 Oxford made him the offer of the living of Burghfield. He was not in two minds in declining; he preferred his plentiful wine, the dry Dublin strands to ride on, his horses and servants and quiet, and the respect he was shown in the Dublin streets. 'The dignity of my present Station damps the pertness of the inferior puppies and Squires, which without plenty and ease on your side of the Channel, would break my heart in a month'; 'like Caesar I will be one of the first here rather than the last among you'.

Swift cannot be said to write with enthusiasm of his domestic life as Dean: but from his *Letters* there emerges a taking picture of it. This is from a letter to Pope, early on, in 1715:

> I live in the corner of a vast unfurnished house; my family consists of a steward, a groom, a helper in the stable, a footman and an old maid, who are all on board wages, and when I do not dine abroad, or make an entertainment (which last is very rare) I eat mutton-pye and drink half a pint of wine'.

From time to time he had a little trouble because the beef-steak was spoiled, the ale sour, Tom the groom too drunk to keep up when out riding, or none of his servants able to read or write properly. This is how he wrote, in 1717, from Trim (he was probably staying with Stella there) to his friend and colleague in Dublin, Thomas Walls the Archdeacon of Achonry:

I shall not have a stocking to my foot, unless Mrs. Brent sends them to you tomorrow and you put them in the Bishop's bag.

Walls was one of his oldest friends – a 'grave and good man', Archbishop King had called him. Swift had known him in Ireland early on (Walls was then a schoolmaster), and again in the London years, when he figures not infrequently in the *Journal to Stella* of 1710-13.

Besides the Deanery itself, Swift had his garden, which he called 'Naboth's Vineyard'. 'I am as busy in my little spot of town garden, as ever I was in the *grand monde*', he wrote in 1723. And above all, he took his exercise, walking and riding. The sight of the elderly Dean, celebrated for harshness towards the great ('I would have your Lordship remember you are to speak to a clergyman, and not to a footman') and gentleness to the poor, became a famous Dublin sight:

> I walk the streets in peace, without being jostled, nor ever without a 1,000 blessings from my friends the vulgar.

That was in 1733. At the same time, one sees the great physical vigour that preserved him, perhaps unhappily, into extreme old age:

> I ride and walk whenever good weather permits, and am reputed the best walker in this Town and 5 miles round.

Swift wrote those words in early 1730. But eight years later there is still the same extraordinary vigour:

> I seldom walk less than 4 miles, sometimes 6 or 8 or 10 or more, never beyond my own limits; or if it rains, I walk as much through the house, up and down stairs.

Riding, his other exercise, still took him out into the Dublin countryside:

> I often ride out in fair weather, with one of my servants laden with a joynt of meat and a bottle of wine, and Town bread, who attends me to some rural parson 5 or 6 miles round this Town.

It is from details like this that, fragment by fragment, one can build up from Swift's *Letters* a picture of his life day by day. In fact they make it possible to do this with a detail and immediacy that has no rival in earlier English letters – of any period – nor in our literature as a whole, until one gets back as far as Ben Jonson, or Shakespeare himself. Why this plain but rich immediacy and detail re-appear with Swift, I hardly know. Perhaps because of his familiar acquaintance with Rabelais. Perhaps because he was the contemporary of Defoe, and lived when the English novel was becoming its true self. The same quality had shown already in some of Swift's poems, like those describing the morning, or a city shower, during his London years.

There went with the Deanship, about 25 miles out in the country from Dublin, the parish of Laracor just south of Trim. Almost the first thing Swift did when he arrived as Dean was to go there. But at that time the parsonage-house was 'of mud and straw', and had gone to ruin into the bargain. His stay there involved him, he records, in 'a field bed and an Earthen floor'; a curious situation, one cannot but reflect, for perhaps the finest mind in the British Isles, and one who only a few months before had been more or less at the heart of public affairs. But Swift liked Laracor: 'My river walk is extremely pretty, and my canal of great Beauty, and I see Trout playing in it'. This was a fortnight after his arrival.

More than this, some of his best friends were close to him in the country. Surviving letters written not by, but to Swift, are testimony to the extraordinarily warm feelings, touched always with respect, that many of the most distinguished men of the day had towards him: and he had many good friends during his Irish years, though some he had to keep close to mainly by letter. There was, for example, John Barber, the printer who was imprisoned in 1714 for bringing out Swift's *Public Spirit of the Whigs*. Barber's wife Mary the poetess, author of *The Widow Gordon's Petition*, reflecting the distress of the poor, was one of the very few women poets whom Swift liked, and may even have slightly admired. Barber went back to London in 1730, when Swift supplied his wife with letters of introduction, and in 1732 he became Lord Mayor. One of Swift's many small actions in advancing those he knew was to persuade the new Lord Mayor to take Matthew Pilkington as chaplain. Charles Boyle, fourth Earl of Orrery, was a good friend of Swift's until his death in 1731, and at about that time Swift got to know his son the fifth Earl. Well enough too, it seems; for in 1736 he was sending the young nobleman an invitation 'commanding' him to dinner at the Deanery; and added, characteristically, 'pray give my Groom a *guinea* for attending you, and for the charges of his Horse'. John Boyle's *Remarks on Swift* of 1751, however, though the first account of him, was an unsympathetic one.

Other friends included John Brandreth, who from 1731 was Dean of Armagh; and Carteret himself, who was Lord Lieutenant from 1724 to 1730 – 'What in God's name do you here? Get back to your own country, and send us our boobies again!' Swift burst out at him once, over some piece of astuteness on Carteret's part that he objected to. Carteret's boast was that when asked what he had done in Ireland, he could answer 'I satisfied Swift!' Until they fell out, there was also Knightley Chetwode, who besides his main property near Portarlington, had another house near Navan. It was only a few miles from Laracor, and Swift visited him there in 1714. At Celbridge, just over the border into Co. Kildare, Vanessa herself had a house, and Swift visited her there too, for example shortly before 1720. Not altogether off the way to it, if one was coming from Dublin, lay Woodpark, the home of Charles Ford, for whom Swift had got the official post of Gazeteer in London in 1712 – he soon lost it, though – and whom he visited at Woodpark in 1723. Then, at Gaulstown, south of Mullingar, was the Rochfort family, whom Swift also visited in the country in 1723. Stella, Chetwode, Canessa, Ford, the Rochforts – or if you like Trim, Celbridge, Woodpark, Gaulstown, Laracor itself – Swift's friends made something of an integrated little world out in the country as well as in Dublin; and one can begin to see a pattern of life for him there also. One of his later friends, William Richardson, had his house far away in the north, at Summerseat near Coleraine. Swift was invited, but it seems that he never managed to go so far. In 1736, Richardson sent him a 27lb salmon, and mentioned in his letter that Swift had promised to come to Summerseat; but that is as far as it went. I shall come back, though, to the Richardsons.

Of course, Swift saw these country friends in Dublin also. So he did others, men like Henry Singleton, the Prime Sergeant from 1726 on, and one of the Dean's executors; or Archdeacon Walls, or one of his closest friends, Patrick Delany, a Junior Fellow at Trinity until 1727. The circle seems to have met sometimes at Delany's house in Stafford St; but Delany also had a house at Glasnevin. Swift's warmest relations, though (in spite of the fact that in the end there was a breach) must have been with Thomas Sheridan. Early on, Sheridan was celebrated as an outstanding Dublin schoolmaster, both classic and mathematician; 'the best Grecian among us', Swift said. He was gay, convivial, improvident, forgetful, scintillating, witty, and richly warm-hearted. Swift loved him well enough to be unusually indulgent towards his faults. 'His greatest fault is a Wife and seven Children'; 'he hath not over-much *Advertency*'; 'if I do not *Sheridan* it, I mean forget it'; 'Sheridan is still the same, as Weathercocks are the same'; 'pray do not employ your time lolling in bed till noon to read Homer'.

Sheridan, however, by marriage to a rich woman, had recovered the family house, which had been forfeited through the family Jacobitism. It was at Quilca, in the poor land of Co. Cavan, and outside the old limit of the Pale, while all the other properties I have mentioned (save of course Summerseat) were within it. In Swift's time – I sometimes wonder if not still a little today – that made a difference. 'I live in a cabin and in a very wild country', Swift wrote of a stay he made at Quilca in 1725. The year before, as a tease, he had started a chronicle called *The Blunders, Deficiencies, Distresses and Misfortunes of Quilca... Proposed to contain One and Twenty Volumes in Quarto*. So there were enough Blunders and Deficiencies for a substantial work. 'But one Lock and a half in the whole House', we read... 'The Kitchen perpetually crowded with Savages... Not a bit of Turf this cold Weather, and Mrs Johnson' – (Stella was there too, then!) – 'and the Dean forc'd to assist at the Bog... the Dean's great Coat was employ'd to stop the wind from coming down the Chimney... the Spit blunted with poking into Bogs for Timber, and tears the Meat into pieces... the Dean deaf and fretting... the *Crew* of Quilca insisting on their right of not milking till eleven in the Forenoon'. Ten years later, in spite of praise for the beef and mutton and inexhaustible supplies of game, life at Quilca – as one might expect – seems not to have much changed:

> But one pair of tongs in the whole house; the turf so wet that a tolerable fire is a miracle; the kitchen in a cabin a hundred feet off; the back and front door always left open, which in a storm (our constant companion) threatens the fall of the whole edifice... but we have a good room to eat in... (and) an honest neighbour Mr. Price, who sits the evening, and wins our money at backgammon.

A racy, detailed first-hand picture emerges of Irish rural life at that time: or, I myself would add, apart from the turf, of rural life in a great many places, today as in Swift's time.

Quilca, however, and Sheridan, had something to offer Swift besides human (if not always material) warmth and hospitality. With Sheridan, Swift's powers of intellect and wit could come at least in large part into play. Indeed, Sheridan, grandfather of the great comic dramatist, sometimes gave Swift as good as he got. One thing he did was to write a Treatise on punning: the letters between them were in fact, often enough, puns a whole letter long: Sheridan writes a string of meaningless gibberish words:

> Yew no eye promise said too right yew a Nun inn tell liege eye bell Let her. He writ is. Eye main ass crop off it.

Fun to look at on the page, but quite hard to read

aloud so that it *doesn't* sound what it is: 'I would have you take some remedies, and then go in a chaise to Wicklow, where I know you will be as welcome as anyone in Ireland. You know I promised to write you an unintelligible letter. Here it is. A scrap of it'. Those last words, I think, show how Sheridan was catching an Irish not an English voice. It makes me think of *Finnegans Wake*, where again, a strong Irish accent very often brings the meaning straight out. They also played the same game in Latin: 'Mire se ver cannas vel res ad a villas a peni' – 'my receiver can as well raise a devil as a penny'. Doubtless Sheridan wrote the truth when he wrote that.

Trifling jests in a way, no doubt: yet important. One may treasure Swift's *Letters* for their racy, intimate domesticity; but after all, Swift is not Parson Woodeford. It was *Gulliver* that he is said to have put the finishing touches to at Quilca. Crucially, one is confronting, in all this, the greatest literary mind of the age as he says (to quote from a letter of 1735), 'thus I patch my life'. In the end, the great quality of the *Letters* is a marvellous gift of language.

Not that, in this, Swift was alone. Those who wrote to him, many of them, also had it – not only the literary men who wrote from London, not only Pope and Arbuthnot and Gay, but also Oxford, Bolingbroke, Bathurst, Peterborough – for the noblemen too, the English of that time could indeed be radiant with vigour, elegance and nicety. None, though, could match Swift in his own two chosen fields. These I see as raillery and simplicity:

> ...to put a stop to this Corruption; and recover the simplicity which in every thing of value ought chiefly to be followed.

Perhaps one thinks that while raillery may need explanation, what simplicity means is simple enough. But in Swift's day, English was like another tongue: richer, crisper, and for the daily affairs of life far stronger that anything at least we English can now make of it. 'It seems there is a trade of carrying stories to the government, and many honest folk *turn the penny* by it'; 'you may count upon it, it lies very much at my heart to make you easy'. Everywhere, finds like these help to make the *Letters* rewarding; and these two, at any rate, one should see as issuing less from the genius of Swift, than from the genius of the language. But they shade into what was his own. 'I never could learn' he writes drily to Arbuthnot in 1734 – Arbuthnot's brother on the continent has sent him some wine – 'what kind of present from here would be acceptable in France'. Behind these seeming-casual words lie not only his periodic outbursts over the 'dirty obscure nook of the world', worse than Hottentot-land, he has to live in (but all these evils are the effects of English tyranny): also his indomitable pillorying of the commercial subjugation whereby Ireland could not export even the few fine things she could produce. One recalls how he sent the first two *Drapier's Letters* to the Lord Lieutenant: 'I have made bold to send you two small tracts... one written (as it is supposed) by the Earl of Abercorn; the other is entitled to a Weaver, and suited to the vulgar, but thought to be the work of a better Hand.'

In these passages, and as I myself believe, always and everywhere, triumph of style is not a knack with words. Behind the sharp edge lies the weight of a great mind and an iron firmness. 'I hope your Lordship', he writes elsewhere, 'who were always so kind to me while you were a servant, will not forget me now in your greatness'. It means the converse of what it seems to mean: the service was the service of the old Queen, the greatness is the exile that comes to patriots in evil times. That was to Bolingbroke. To Oxford, just after his release from the Tower, he wrote: 'this glorious scene of your life (I do not mean your Discharge, but your... Imprisonment)'. In Ireland, I suppose, those words might have overtones that it hardly falls to me to underline.

Grand as it is, it is not quite on this note that I should wish to close. There is another side: the domestic Dean whom I have tried also to depict. And it is in these more relaxed and intimate contexts that Swift's raillery appears. Raillery, to praise by seeming blame, or more generally, to make oneself amiable through the seeming converse of amiability, was one of Swift's special loves. It could express at once the kindliness, and the rebarbativeness of his nature; and beyond that it is a great and subtle compliment to the hearer, a major act of trust both in his intelligence, and in his nearness of feeling to you. 'I begged some mutton of you, and you put me off with a barrel of ale, these disappointments we must bear'; that's what

Swift writes to his colleague at St. Patrick's, the Reverend John Blatchford, in 1731. Here is how, irresistibly to my mind, he shows his special warmth for Archdeacon Wells:

> This letter is to go to the Bishop of Clogher on Saturday, and should have gone last night, if I had not thought you might be such a fool as to copy it today and send it to the Bishop of Dromore likewise. If you will come this morning and do it here we will dine together... If there be a greater fool than I who took Pains to write it, it must be he who copies it out. Adieu.

And as late as 1738, this immortal letter is how he can repay Richardson's daughter Katharine, who had made him a half-dozen of shirts:

> Madam,
>
> I must begin my correspondence by letting you know that your uncle is the most unreasonable person I was ever acquainted with; and next to him you are the second, although I think impartially that you are worse than he... I find you follow in your uncle's footsteps, by maliciously bribing a useless man, who can never have it in his power to serve or divert you... Your uncle came to me several times; and I believe after several invitations, dined with me once or twice. This was all the provocation I ever gave him; but he had revenge in his breast, and you shall hear how he gratified it. First, he was told, that my ill stomach... forced me... to take a

spoonful of usquebaugh: he discovered where I bought it, and sent me a dozen bottles... He next... found out the merchant with whom I deal, by the treachery of my butler, and sent me twelve dozen bottles of (sweet Spanish wine)... But what can I say of a man, who, some years before I ever saw him, was loading me every season with salmons, that surfeited myself and all my visitors? Whereby it is plain that his malice reached to my friends as well as myself. And last, to complete his ill designs, he must needs force his neice into the plot; because it can be proved... that you have been his partaker and second in mischief, by sending me half a dozen of shirts, although I never once gave you the least cause of displeasure. And what is yet worse, the few ladies that come to the Deanery assure me, that they never saw so fine linen, or better worked up, or more exactly fitted. It is a happiness they were not stockings, for then you would have known the length of my foot... I have seen some persons who live in your neighbourhood... but I found you had bribed them all, by never sending them any such dangerous presents: For they swore to me, that you were a lady adorned with all perfections, such as virtue, prudence, wit, humour, excellent conversation, and even good housewifery; which last is seldom the talent of ladies of this kingdom. But I take so ill your manner of treating me, that I shall not believe one syllable of what they said, until I have it by letter under your own hand.

It is not Swift's best letter of raillery. He was 71, and

ill. But when one finds he could write a private letter like that, one's mind goes back to the great loss and waste in all these years of 'patching life':

> I write pamphlets and follys meerly for amusement, and when they are finished, or as I grow weary in the middle, I cast them into the fire, partly out of dislike, and chiefly because I know they will signify nothing.

So in 1730. That, again, is the other side. And there, all in all, is the complex balance of his Irish years; one that goes back right to the beginning, to that evening of the 10th of June 1713, when the newly-appointed Dean of St. Patrick's stepped off the packet from England.

Swift as Poet

by DENIS DONOGHUE

When we say that Swift was an occasional poet or even an amateur we mean that he took his poetry with less gravity than his prose. But we mean a little more than that. It is true that many of his poems give the impression of being vacation exercises: he carried his verses lightly, and put them aside with equal nonchalance. If the poems turned out well, he was pleased to discover their merit, but he did not demand such returns. Indeed, the most useful service offered him by the existence of poetry was that it helped him to deal with certain modes of experience in an undemanding spirit. There are a few poems in which he is as severe as ever, full of indignation and demand. The voice we hear is an echo of the voice in the *Tale of a Tub* and *Gulliver's Travels*. But these are exceptional occasions. Most of Swift's poems are more equable than his prose, more urbane in their relationships: they have the effect of releasing him, now and again, from his quarrel with the world. Even when the quarrel persists in the poems, it is free from the desperation of the prose, the sense of inevitable defeat. Indeed, there were many aspects of life which Swift could hardly have borne at all, but for the amateur nature of his poetry. He wrote poetry for ease, to lift the strain.

There is some reason to think that his poems helped to keep him sane by protecting him from the edge of crisis. Or so I would suggest.

It is clear that many of the poems were written for fun. But fun, to Swift, was an athletic exercise to keep the mind in trim. A riddle, a lampoon, anything would serve. If he could turn a local irritation into verse, he could rid himself of the bitterness attending it. When Thomas Rundle was appointed Bishop of Derry in February, 1735, Swift resented the appointment largely, it seems, because Rundle was sponsored by the Lord Chancellor. So he wrote a skit on the Bishop and disposed of his resentment in sixty lines. A few months later he wrote a glowing account of Rundle's merits in a letter to Alexander Pope.

In 1934 W. B. Yeats told Oliver Edwards that in poetry he took his later manner from Swift. And then, for proof and illustration, he read the third stanza of Swift's *Ode to the honourable Sir William Temple*:

> But what does our proud Ign'rance Learning call,
>   We oddly Plato's paradox make good,
> Our Knowledge is but mere Remembrance all,
>   Remembrance is our Treasure and our Food;
> Nature's fair Table-book our tender Souls
> We scrawl all o'er with old and empty Rules,
>   Stale Memorandums of the Schools;
>   For Learning's mighty Treasures look
>   In that deep Grave a Book,
>   Think she there does all her Treasures hide,
> And that her troubled Ghost still haunts there since
>   she dy'd,

Confine her walks to Colleges and Schools,
    Her priests, her Train and Followers show
    As if they all were Spectres too,
    They purchase Knowledge at the Expense
    Of common Breeding, common Sense,
    And at once grow Scholars and Fools;
    Affect ill-manner'd Pedantry,
Rudeness, Ill-Nature, Incivility,
    And sick with Dregs of Knowledge grown,
    Which greedily they swallow down,
    Still cast it up and nauseate Company.

This comes from one of Swift's earliest poems. We are accustomed to think of it as mere 'prentice work'. Readers who seldom agree on anything come together in this opinion. But if we read the Ode again with Yeats in mind, we see that the young Swift is not shamed by that relation. There are many rough patches in the poem, but there are other places in which the poet has something of that vigour, that directness, which we admire in Yeats's later work. Yeats did not tell Oliver Edwards what he admired in the Ode. When he quoted the same stanza again, in a vivid paragraph of his pamphlet *On the Boiler*, he gave it without comment. But we can guess that what he admired was a certain high tone, a certain splendour. We hear it in the juxtaposition of 'common Breeding, common Sense'; before that, in the invocation to Learning's 'troubled Ghost'; and further back still, in the scrawling of Nature's table-book. If we think of this as a Yeatsian tone, we mark the strength of the tradition he invoked: to a large extent it is Swift's tradition, tuned for a new context. The values to which Swift appeals in the Ode are Yeatsian values; Nature, civility, courtesy, a certain independence of spirit. The poem implies that they are still available, though they are increasingly under attack. Swift invokes these values, but if necessary he will speak upon his own authority. This is what we mean when he think of him as a great Augustan writer. One of the most engaging marks of Augustan literature is its commitment to one thing at a time. The poet does not claim to say everything at once, in one poem, one book, one word. He confronts every occasion as it arises. Much of 19th century poetry is so grandiose in its intention that it is unwilling to say one thing at a time. It resents this limitation. The Augustan poet takes it as a matter of course: I am sure that it is the source of that directness which is so admirable in Swift's poems. In September, 1727, Swift was delayed a week at Holyhead while coming back to Dublin. He was deeply concerned about Stella, who was ill. During those days, while he had nothing better to do, he kept a diary and scribbled verses as they occurred to him. One of them begins:

Lo here I sit at holy head
With muddy ale and mouldy bread
All Christian vittals stink of fish
I'm where my enemyes would wish.

It is easy to say that this is not great poetry and that

it is close to doggerel: but it is more important to recognise the continuity between Swift's doggerel and his greatest work; that the imaginative resilience of the one depends upon the vigour of the other, the readiness to speak out. The sense of 'muddy ale and mouldy bread' animates the great occasions in *Gulliver's Travels*, the *Modest Proposal*, the *Description of the Morning*, and all the other choice things. There are certain tones in poetry which depend upon that sense; tones which are not available in more sublime poems. Yeats discovered this when he wrote the occasional poems in his own *Responsibilities* and *The green Helmet*.

Swift did not, of course, strike this note as soon as he took to verse. Largely under the influence of Cowley, he stuck to the Ode, for his first poems, and the Ode was an intractable form. He had very little feeling for this form, and as long as he clung to it, he established only a fitful relation with his true concerns. To hear Swift going through the motions of an Ode is to mark a certain ventriloquism in his style. A modern philosopher speaks of a vocation of mind. There is a kind of destiny in these matters. The form of the Ode was intractable to Swift because it had little to do with the chief qualities of his mind. The Ode spreads itself over a long stanza, the lines unequal, the rhythm resisting definition at any point. It delights in postponement. If the lines are not to flag, they must aspire, and the poet must go along with the 'excelsior' note and whatever it entails. It is hard to be your own master in the Ode. Swift is uncomfortable in this restriction. His mind works best in the juxtaposition of small units, in strict balance and adjudication, where every change of direction is under minute control. He does not like to wait to see what is going to develop. As a poet he distrusts the vague, transitional moments, when a thing is neither completely itself nor something else. He is restless with things that do not declare their own identity. In the poem called *The Day of Judgement* he speaks of 'the World's mad Business', and to Swift the main forms of that madness were abstraction, formlessness, bogus visions, clouds of human pride. Poems were worthwhile because they were receptacles of sense; specific things. They were ways of getting things done. In the poem *Verses on the Death of Dr. Swift*, he praises Pope, as Shenstone would praise him later, for putting an uncommon amount of sense into his lines:

> In Pope, I cannot read a line,
> But with a Sigh, I wish it mine:
> When he can in one Couplet fix
> More Sense than I can do in six.

What he means by 'sense' is clear enough; thoughts that have survived the trial of experience. It is clearer still when he puts it beside a word like 'true'. In his Imitation of Horace's *Hoc erat in votis* Swift says:

> And let me in these Shades compose
> Something in Verse as true as Prose;
> Remov'd from all th' ambitious Scene
> Nor puff'd by Pride, nor sunk by Spleen.

So the 'sin of wit' which he invoked in another poem means the unpopular force of intelligence, truth, sense, the sharp edge of discrimination. Swift is not interested in daring flights of fancy on which new meanings may be discovered. He distrusts every ambiguous cloud of significance. He is content with the old meanings, and angry that they are denied; poetry is a way of maintaining their force. This is what he means by 'fixing' the sense.

Obviously, among the available literary forms, he needed the couplet: if it did not exist, he would have had to invent it. The couplet allows Swift to direct a flow of energy through single meanings and finite relationships. This is a prior condition before there can be any general significance at all; since general significance, to Swift, is merely the sum of specific acts of intelligence. In this sense Swift is a 'literalist of the imagination': the facility provided by the couplet is that it requires the deployment of specific meanings, moment by moment: every shot has to count. The result is that the double vocation of mind and form enabled him to hold at bay themes which, in the prose, threatened to run wild. In poems like *The Beasts' Confession* and *On Poetry*: A *Rhapsody* Swift curbs the same themes which, in prose, drive him into the violence of *Gulliver's Travels*; the couplet gives him the assurance that control is still possible. In the Rhapsody he says:

> What Reason can there by assign'd
> For this Perverseness in the Mind?
> Brutes find out where their Talents lie:

A Bear will not attempt to fly:
A founder'd Horse will oft debate
Before he tries a five-barr'd Gate:
A Dog by Instinct turns aside,
Who sees the Ditch too deep and wide.
But Man we find the only Creature,
Who, led by Folly, fights with Nature;
Who, when she loudly cries, Forbear,
With Obstinacy fixes there;
And, where his Genius least inclines,
Absurdly bends his whole Designs.

If the tone is rueful, it is still safe. One reason for this urbanity, in a writer to whom urbanity comes hard, is that in English literature the tradition in which such comment is securely made is largely a poetic tradition. The serious part of the tradition issues in the satires of Dryden and Pope; the burlesque part issues in Butler and John Philips. Swift could choose; the conventions were well established. In prose fiction the lines were not at all as clear; it was much harder to imagine how the thing might be done. The tradition of English verse satire, going back from Pope and Dryden through Donne, Ralegh, and Greville to Lyndsay, the Scottish satirists, and beyond, was a more complete accomplishment; it was in close relation to the great dramatic tragedies, for one thing. Swift was a direct heir to this tradition and in using it he could take the weight of its authority.

So he confronts the incorrigible themes with vigour and resource which are partly personal and partly traditional. The themes are those which irritate the prose; it is still the old, inescapable story – the vanity of human delusion, the decay of intelligence. The concern which reverberates through the poems is the fear that intelligence is beaten, that the enemies are already at the gate. The chief enemy is what Marshall McLuhan calls 'the slagheap of the unconscious,' the realm of Chaos and 'old Night' invoked in Pope's *Dunciad*. Pope and Swift are determined to force things into the light of day. Swift goes even further than Pope in exposing whatever is dark or subliminal. So that even when he writes an occasional poem, he is always keeping his mind focussed on the main job; to push things into the daylight of commonsense, to force them into definition.

Already in Swift's day this seemed a last-minute attempt to hold the fort. One of the most remarkable developments in 18th century literature is that within 25 years after the publication of the *Dunciad* the slagheap of the unconscious would be considered the chief source of poetic vision. The crucial term in this story is Imagination; in the first years of the 18th century it was still considered a wild and unreliable power. But by the middle of the century it had been promoted. Thomas Warton objects to Pope's poetry precisely because it lives in a world of sunlight, the world of the understanding, rather than the more subtle twilight of the imagination. Indeed, when Pope used images of darkness and night to represent the loss of clarity, form, and intelligence, he stood on ground which was shifting beneath his feet. Within a remarkably short time these images would acquire a new and paradoxical 'radiance'; the most profound visions were now available, it seemed, at night, and the moon took the place of the sun as the visionary power. The new suggestion is that the effect of the white light of Reason is to enforce the separation of man from Nature. The light of reconciliation is twilight. Along with this, there is a new assumption, that the crucial events take place within the mind; not outside. Nothing could be more alien to Swift. He would not speak the new language. To him, what happened inside the mind, in most cases, was mere delusion. The important events were public, social, and political. When Yeats wrote of 'the Tragic Generation' he found that one of the causes of its tragedy was the morbid effort to create a new kind of purity from images, as he said, more and more separated from 'the general purposes of life'. These general purposes are the aims of man in society. To a writer like Swift they are the only purposes worth talking about. Swift and Pope spent their lives attending to those purposes: choosing, adjusting, discriminating, bringing some things forward, casting other things down. They worked on the assumption that if the social aims of man are clarified and tested, his private aims will look after themselves. The immediate necessity was to enlarge the domain of mind and intelligence. If something has to be rejected, well and good, let it be rejected; but keep the slagheap of the unconscious as small as possible.

Sometimes the way to do it was by direct attack –

invective. Perhaps the finest example of this in Swift is the poem, *The Legion Club*: an attack upon the members of the Irish House of Commons when they had voted to deprive the clergy of certain tithes legally due. The poem is called *The Legion Club* because of the answer of the unclean spirit in *St. Mark*: 'My name is Legion; for we are many'. This prompts Swift to develop the notion that the members of the House are all mad, that the House itself is Bedlam: or again, that the House is Hell, full of evil shadows and spirits. Or a cage for weird animals. In one stanza he dreams of destroying the House, with the Devil's aid, on the understanding that God often uses the Devil as His scourge, punishing the wicked. But then he thinks of letting the House stand and using it as a lunatic asylum. He plays this idea for all it is worth

Since the House is like to last,
Let a royal Grant be pass'd,
That the Club have Right to dwell
Each within his proper Cell;
With a Passage left to creep in,
And a Hole above for peeping.
  Let them, when they once get in
Sell the Nation for a pin;
While they sit a-picking Straws
  Let them rave of making Laws;
While they never hold their Tongue
Let them dabble in their Dung;
Let them form a grand Committee,
How to plague and starve the City;

And so it goes on. It could go on indefinitely. The first effect of the couplets is to ensure that they command whatever they touch. Very often this is a matter of bringing images into startling relationships. The relation between 'picking Straws' and 'making Laws', for instance, is a brilliant parody of choice and chance, achieved with the connivance of an accommodating language. This is what Swift means when, in another poem, he speaks of 'my own hum'rous biting way'. It is his 'sin of wit'.

But this is only one of Swift's procedures. Very often his method is raillery. Sometimes he takes his enemy at his word, and shows what a silly word it is. Or again he shows what happens if you take something literally which is meant to be metaphorical. In *The Progress of Beauty* he makes fun of beauty by taking literally the romantic comparison between a beautiful face and the Moon: as the Moon wanes, the beautiful Celia declines. In the 'boudoir' poems Swift treats the organic as if it were mechanical. But always, in these poems, poetry is the pressure of a detached intelligence applied to our delusions and myths. If we insist upon our folly, Swift implies, we must take the consequences. At least, after the poem, we cannot plead innocent. Wherever good sense is in danger, especially if the danger comes from our pride, Swift is on hand to defend the right. The intelligent life is an endless war against absurdity, pretention, the unconscious, darkness. Swift tries to rid the world of anything that does not survive the test of daylight and intelligence. One of his greatest poems in this way is called *On*

Dreams. I will give the first few stanzas:

Those Dreams that on the silent Night intrude,
And with false flitting Shades our Minds delude,
Jove never sends us downward from the Skies,
Nor can they from infernal Mansions rise;
But all are meer Productions of the Brain,
And Fools consult Interpreters in vain.

For, when in Bed we rest our weary Limbs,
The Mind unburthen'd sports in various Whims,
The busy Head with mimick Art runs o'er
The Scenes and Actions of the Day before.

The drowsy Tyrant, by his Minions led,
To regal Rage devotes some Patriot's Head,
With equal Terrors, not with equal Guilt,
The Murd'rer dreams of all the Blood he spilt.

The Soldier smiling hears the Widow's Cries,
And stabs the Son before the Mother's Eyes.
With Remorse his Brother of the Trade,
The Butcher, feels the Lamb beneath his blade.

It is typical of Swift to put the blame on man himself. Dreams are not sent from Heaven, or even from Hell; we ourselves devise them, they are functions of our own corruption. In another poem, *A beautiful young Nymph going to Bed*, there is the same implication, that dreams follow the nature of the dreamer. Dreams delude our minds by setting before us our own fancies, memories, and desires; an unwholesome compound from which we extract our visions. The only difference, Swift implies, between the dream and the reality is that in the dream-world we pursue our desires with impunity; in the real world, at least up to now and for the moment, there are a few obstacles in our way. This tension between the real world, where our corruption is held in restraint, and the dream-world, in which we act as viciously as our desires, accounts for the weight of Swift's satire. Mostly, the satire works by similarity beneath overt difference; as the dreams of the soldier and the butcher are shown to be identical. It is the same force that, in another stanza, associates the physician with the hangman. The soldier smiles when he hears the widow crying, and to round out the symmetry of the occasion waits for the mother to see him before he stabs the son. There are suggestions here of a grisly decorum. The butcher's performance lacks an audience of this splendour, but he makes up for it by relishing the first gesture; nothing as detached as seeing his victim, he 'feels' the lamb beneath his blade. By the time we reach this stage in the poem, the whole inner landscape has been taken over by demons, a weird Dance of Death.

I should not imply that Swift's poems are all in this vein. He had light moments, when the easy occasion called for the other kind of wit; poems like *Mrs. Harris's Petition*. Indeed, to go through Swift's entire poetry is to be astonished by its variety, the range of feeling invoked. We often think that of all the different kinds of poetry, he wrote only two or three; but we forget the occasions when the writing of a poem served instead of a letter, a pun, a conversation, a journey, or a speech in the House of Commons. To open the *Collected Poems* at random is a good method of testing our impression of his poetry; and often we find that our impression is too narrow. Here are a few lines come upon in this way:

By Faction tir'd, with Grief he waits a while
His great contending Friends to reconcile.
Performs what Friendship, Justice, Truth require;
What could he more, but decently retire?

If we didn't know, it would be hard to ascribe that to Swift; at least with any conviction. The tone seems more delicate, more charitable, than our standard impression of him. But we must allow for it. Swift wrote the poem, *The Author upon Himself*, in the summer of 1714, in distress at the growing bitterness between his great contending friends Oxford and Bolingbroke.

But if we take from the poems a single image; what emerges is the image of the poet, embattled, on the last ditch. I have remarked that he used the resources of a great poetic tradition, but that is cold comfort if the poet knows that the tradition is on the way out, that the values by which he lived are doomed. We find something of this again in Yeats: it was Yeats who said, looking toward our own day, 'After us the Savage God'. It is an apocalyptic vision, Swiftian in its way.

MORE MERCIER BOOKS

THE FORTUNES OF THE IRISH LANGUAGE

Daniel Corkery **5/-**

Irish is a Celtic language; its closest relation being the Gaelic of Scotland and Manx. Welsh, Armorican and Cornish are also Celtic languages, but not so closely related. Irish literature existed perhaps for a thousand years before 700 A.D. but no written specimens remain.

When Henry VIII's scheme to de–Irelandise Ireland was begun; land language and religion were his three obstacles. A systematic assault on the language and its institutions was begun. But it was the refusal of the Gaels to really be under which decided that the living Irish tradition was eventually to fall into the custody of the common people of Ireland – tillers of the soil.

IRISH FIRESIDE FOLKTALES

Patrick Kennedy **Volume I. 6/-**

The art of storytelling has been richly developed in Ireland, and through the centuries generations of storytellers have handed down folktales of all kinds.

Patrick Kennedy was born in 1801 in a small village in Wexford. He grew up among the peasantry, and later became a bookseller in Dublin.

In his writing, he embodied oral lore, customs and beliefs that had been current during his youth.

SHORT STORIES OF PADRAIC PEARSE

translated by Desmond Maguire **8/6**

Padraic Pearse, who played a prominent part in the 1916 Rebellion, declared Ireland a Republic from the steps of the General Post Office in Dublin just over fifty years ago. He was executed, along with the other leaders, for his part in the Rising.

These five stories show us that Pearse was a man of deep understanding. He analyses the sorrows and joys of the Irish people of his time, and writes of the tragedies of life and death from which they could never escape.

THE STORMY HILLS

Daniel Corkery **6/-**

Daniel Corkery, one of the most notable influences on Irish fiction, shared the faith and sensitivity of his people. These are stories of great force and atmosphere. They tell of life in a mountainy landscape and of man's struggle with the land. They are stories of people caught in the net of hardship and passion – with the pounding of the sea, the lonely hills, and fields abandoned to nature.

THE LIFE AND DEATH OF MICHAEL COLLINS

Eoin Neeson **hardcover. approx. 30/-**

Although Michael Collins was probably the most dynamic Irish political personality of his age, who still commands loyalties and allegiances, provokes argument as emphatic as when he was alive almost two generations ago, the popular image of him is extremely distorted.

This book examines in detail the fatal ambush at Beal na mBlath, and considers not alone what Collins' problems were and how he faced them, but why he faced them in the way he did, and what the outcome was.

THE PATH TO FREEDOM

Michael Collins **6/-**

Challenging, vital, brilliant and sensitive, Michael Collins has become almost a legendary figure, and even today his tragic death is still the subject of discussion and speculation. These articles and speeches, first published in 1922, are written in a forceful and very personal style in which he evaluates our heritage, puts forward his arguments in favour of the Treaty, and shows the possibilities for an Ireland of the future.

THE HEDGE SCHOOLS OF IRELAND

P. J. Dowling **6/-**

This book opens with a brief historical account of education in Ireland to the middle of the seventeenth century. The story of the Hedge Schools may be said to date from this time; but it was in the eighteenth century that they really took root. Some schools taught classics and mathematics; others, only reading, writing and arithmetic.

A schoolmaster had occasionally to undergo a long and arduous training as a 'poor scholar'. Some few schoolmasters were poets; others were scholars of considerable reputation.

IRISH REGIMENTS IN THE FIRST WORLD WAR

Henry Harris **hardcover. approx. 40/-**

This book tells for the first time the story of the Irish regiments in the British Army in the Great War. England has remembered them, and so has France. But Ireland chose to forget these men until, on the eve of the Rising Commemoration in 1966, when the then Taoiseach, Sean Lemass, in the presence of President De Valera, gave credit long due to the tens of thousands of Irishmen who gave their lives for the cause of freedom.

The author is a retired British Army officer already well-known in Irish historical circles.

The Thomas Davis Lectures in paperback

First published in the Netherlands
Made and printed by Bosch, Utrecht